THE
Fingerless Lady
LIVING IN MY HEAD

*One Guy's Musings
About Tolerance*

DON EVERTS

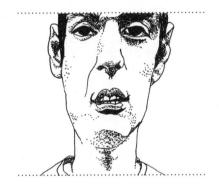

IVP Books

An imprint of InterVarsity Press
Downers Grove, Illinois

InterVarsity Press
P.O. Box 1400, Downers Grove, IL 60515-1426
World Wide Web: www.ivpress.com
E-mail: email@ivpress.com

InterVarsity Press® is the book-publishing division of InterVarsity Christian Fellowship/USA®, a student movement active on campus at hundreds of universities, colleges and schools of nursing in the United States of America, and a member movement of the International Fellowship of Evangelical Students. For information about local and regional activities, write Public Relations Dept., InterVarsity Christian Fellowship/USA, 6400 Schroeder Rd., P.O. Box 7895, Madison, WI 53707-7895, or visit the IVCF website at <www.intervarsity.org>.

Illustrations and design by Matt Smith

ISBN 978-0-8308-3614-7

Printed in the United States of America ∞

Library of Congress Cataloging-in-Publication Data

Everts, Don, 1971-
    The fingerless lady living in my head: one guy's musing about tolerance / Don Everts.
      p. cm.—(One guy's head)
    Includes bibliographical references.
    ISBN-13: 978-0-8308-3614-7 (pbk.: alk. paper)
    1. Christianity—Philosophy—Miscellanea. 2. Philosophy and religion—Miscellanea. 3. Toleration—Religious aspects—Christianity—Miscellanea. I. Title.
    BR100.E942007
    230—dc22

                        2007031476

P	15	14	13	12	11	10	9	8	7	6	5	4	3	2	1
Y	19	18	17	16	15	14	13	12	11	10	09	08	07		

Contents

INTRODUCTION:
MY HEAD

Welcome to my head.

In the following pages I plan to introduce you to some of the various ideas that live up in my head, and you'll have the pleasure of meeting one idea up there in particular. That idea tends to act like a very nice lady who happens to have no fingers on her hands. Just thumbs and odd-looking stubs where her fingers used to be. She's a popular lady and she roams around my head in a long, kindergarten-teacher kind of dress. She's always smiling and very kind to the other ideas living in my head. But there is something creepy about those hands of hers. Tolerance is the name you might know her by, but THE FINGERLESS LADY is what the rest of the ideas up in my head call her.

But I'm getting ahead of myself. Before you

meet this one idea, I think it's important to let you
know why anyone should care about my head at all.

For the full answer, you'd really have to go on
the full tour of my head.[1] But for now let me just say
that my goal for trying to honestly describe what
goes on up in my head (a potentially embarrassing
endeavor) is not to provide some sort of intellectual peep show. It's really not. My first goal is to
honestly describe what I believe about tolerance—
and how I go about believing it. My second goal is
to encourage more honest self-reflection and more
relaxed conversations among people with heads
full of different ideas. My hope is that my own hon-
esty will help us all (myself included) practice the
exquisite, everyday, joyful art of thinking more and
more all the time.

That's why I'm letting you take a trip into my
head to meet THE FINGERLESS LADY. But before
we get to the formal introductions, I should prob-
ably give you a peek into how things generally
work up there in my head, so that this introduc-
tion of THE FINGERLESS LADY makes at least a little sense to you.

Up in my head, ideas walk around like people.

Some folks say that ideas are inert propositional
statements and that thinking is like doing science
or math: you judge and weigh pieces of data until
you find out what's consistent and true. Other
folks say that ideas are more like snatches of vis-

ceral experience and that thinking is the act of honestly feeling these subjective experiences.

But when I am honest with myself, I have to admit that the ideas up in my head aren't quite so cold and datalike as some say, nor as subjective and experiential as others say. In my head, ideas tend to act more like people: they each have their own personality, their own style, their own way of getting along in my head. And each of them has a story to tell me.

For example, it's not like THE FINGERLESS LADY is a dispassionate propositional statement about truth and tolerance waiting to be examined or some existentially honest experience waiting to be felt. It's like that idea is really up there. It has a personality and acts like . . . well, in this case, like a nice woman with no fingers. A fingerless lady who has a story to tell.

THE FINGERLESS LADY isn't alone, of course. There are all kinds of ideas living up there in this house of living ideas. And each one has its own story. Some have been up there since I was a kid (such as THE GOLD OF BOOKS, who tells a story about how great it is to be a reader); others are new ideas that walked into my head recently when I was reading a new book (for example, SHINY HAPPY GLOBALIZATION, who tells a story about the upside of our increasingly global economies and technologies).

That's what ideas are like up in my head. Thinking, then, is when I call a house meeting and all of the ideas (well, most of them) come to the living room in my head. The living room is where the ideas hang out together, tell their stories to each other, ask questions, argue, fight, agree and so on. Stuff you would do if you lived in a house with a bunch of other people and hung out together in the living room. When the ideas are interacting with each other in the living room—I'm thinking.

Sounds a bit chaotic, I guess. But if you've ever lived in a crowded house with a bunch of other people, you know very well that every house wants order. This order doesn't have to be explicit *(George is in charge!),* but it is definite *(George is a fifth-year senior?! I guess he gets the big bedroom, huh?).*

As in any real house, the house of living ideas in my head has social hierarchies (some ideas have been around longer and hold more sway), tensions (some new ideas that walk into my head aren't liked by anyone else and are eventually kicked right out of my head) and complexities (not all the stories perfectly jibe, which means the ideas have some talking to do if they plan to live in the same head together). This is why getting the ideas to interact in the living room (thinking) is so crucial (and, usually, quite interesting).

Anyway, up in my head there is this one idea called, simply, THE FINGERLESS LADY. She roams around pleasantly, speaking kindly to most of the other ideas. She smiles a lot and always gives other ideas a big, encouraging thumbs-up sign—which looks mighty weird on account of her having no other fingers. And she loves to tell her story, just like every other idea. And she has quite a story to tell about tolerance.

But how did she get up there in the first place? And what, exactly, is her story? And what does she have to say for herself when other ideas start peppering her with questions? And, in the end, am I really going to let her stay living up there in my head?

Well, those questions are what this book is all about. Which means it's time to get on with the introductions. If you turn the page, you can enter my house of living ideas and meet this popular idea for yourself.

MEET THE
FINGERLESS LADY

There is a fingerless lady that visits my head from time to time.

You can't miss her.

When I first met her (I think I was reading the Letters to the Editor section of my local paper when this idea first walked into my head), she flashed me the biggest smile and gave me a huge thumbs-up sign. Her eyes were calm and reassuring. And she had a kind, tender way about her. She spoke softly and I felt tranquil in her presence.

But while this initial meeting should have encouraged me and made me feel nice and warm inside, instead I found myself a bit put off.

I didn't know why I felt weird around this new idea at first. And I felt a bit guilty that her warm welcome didn't completely endear her to me and put me at ease. She was wearing a kindergarten-teacher dress, after all. You know the kind of dress

I'm talking about, right? One of those floor-length, quilted-looking dresses that you just have to be a nice, warm, caring woman in order to wear? This new idea was wearing one of those dresses. Everything about her was calm and warm and encouraging. There was nothing in her eyes but welcome and acceptance.

But after spending some time with her, and seeing her give her thumbs-up to more and more ideas in my head, it hit me: her hands were mutilated. As I looked closer at this idea, I saw that all her fingers had been cut off. Only the two thumbs and a bunch of scars were left.

Yes, her hands are all stubs. And thumbs. (It really is rather gross to stare at her hands for long, I found out.)

This mutilation is, of course, puzzling to me and to most of the ideas she comes into contact with up in my head. She's a talkative idea and tends to get lots of attention when she's interacting with other ideas up in my head. But while her voice is calm and she is encouraging to be around, many of the ideas living up in my head eventually find themselves wondering what could have happened to her fingers and why she gives that thumbs-up to everyone. So who cut off her eight fingers? And did it hurt? And why is she still smiling? And why is her smile so . . . *big*?

Lots of questions. But the good news is, she's an

idea. Which means she has a story to tell. And since she's so popular, she actually gets a fair amount of airtime when she's up there in my head. So there's plenty of opportunity for her to tell her story.

And as she tells her story about tolerance in that soothing voice of hers and interacts with the other, often less popular, ideas up in my head, I get a sense of what this idea is all about and what happened to her fingers.

THE FINGERLESS LADY has a wonderful voice and is pleasant to listen to. And I have ample opportunities to do just that. She's an idea, after all. And every idea has a story to tell.

Chapter 2

THE FINGERLESS
LADY'S STORY

THE FINGERLESS LADY, with her smiles and thumbs-up gestures, enjoys telling her story to the other ideas living up in my head. You can tell she's used to telling her story—she's got it down pat. And you can tell she's used to getting a positive response to her story.

Her voice is interesting. It's kind and careful and measured and sugary. The kind of voice you hear on instructional videos sometimes. A little too careful and too measured for my own tastes. But I imagine she'd do just fine filling in as a guest on the *Barney* show, if you see what I mean. And in that compelling voice she tells this story . . .

"Once I was hiking around a mountain. A big mountain—Mount Rainier, in fact. Mount Rainier is an unbelievably beautiful mountain outside Tacoma, Washington. Isn't nature just wonderful?

"Anyway, I was on a long trail that encircled the

mountain. This trail is called the Wonderland Trail, and it is just that: full of wonder! I was on an expedition to hike the trail all the way around the mountain. This long hike would take my friends and me about seven days to complete. Can you imagine the beauty and wonder of hiking such a long way around Mount Rainier?

"Well, as my hiking party and I started out, we were on the south side of the mountain. And as we continued clockwise, we saw the west side of the mountain and then moved on to the north and, eventually, around to the rest of the mountain as well. We walked in a complete circle around Mount Rainier. A circle full of wonder.

"And we noticed an interesting thing as we hiked: the mountain looked different every day."

She pauses a moment for effect, and only after looking around at the other ideas in my head and making meaningful eye contact does she continue.

"In fact, even from the morning to the afternoon we would see many different aspects of the mountain. One morning we saw only the tall sharp-rocked cliffs of the Tatoosh Range on Mount Rainier's south side. But later we could see more of the white, expansive glaciers on the mountain's upper regions. One afternoon we couldn't see the peak at all, for we were in a little valley on the mountain's side. We were surrounded by waterfalls and brightly colored Indian Paintbrush flowers and lush ferns and moss-covered rocks."

At this point many of the ideas in my head lean forward and seem quite taken by the story. THE BEAUTY OF NATURE is nodding in agreement. And LUST FOR ADVENTURE is getting a faraway look in his eyes. Smiling at them all and nodding, THE FINGERLESS LADY continues in her careful voice.

"If you had asked us to describe the mountain on our first day, you would have gotten a very different description than if you asked us on our second day. On our first day Mount Rainier was a mountain of steep cliffs, sharp rocks, precarious ridges and amazing, almost terrifying vistas!

"But on the second day we saw a different part of Mount Rainier. On that day Mount Rainier was a mountain of long, soft, sloped snow fields. It almost looked like ice cream. Ice cream spread between the gray rocks and green trees.

"And our honest descriptions of Mount Rainier each day would have been just as varied and diverse as the many faces of the mountain itself."

She pauses again and smiles, looking into the eyes of the ideas sitting nearest to her in the living room. LUST FOR ADVENTURE is smiling broadly, imagining this great mountain. THE BEAUTY OF NATURE is practically dancing to her words as she continues.

"You might even be tempted to wonder, based on our different descriptions, if we were indeed describing a single mountain. Were we seeing the same mountain each day? Or were these different mountains?" Her voice rises a bit here, as if she's worried. But she doesn't look worried at all, and she continues in her painfully calm voice.

"Were we seeing the same mountain? Of course. You see, as we hiked around Mount Rainier, we realized the Truth about Mountains.

"The Truth about Mountains is that they are so large and so varied that one can get a rich spectrum of perspectives on each mountain. How could something so beautiful and mammoth and teeming with life ever be adequately summed up from only one perspective?

"What is Mount Rainier? Well, that depends on where you happen to be standing, doesn't it?

"And this isn't just the Truth about Mountains; it is the truth about so much in life. What is love? What is peace? What is fairness? What is justice? We all stand somewhere different and therefore have different perspectives. There is no 'right' or 'wrong' perspective. We all stand where we stand and see what we see."

At this point PERSPECTIVE IS EVERYTHING begins to nod softly, her eyes almost closed in rapturous thoughts. PERSPECTIVE IS EVERYTHING is an elegant idea that wears jewelry from around the world, dangling jewelry that makes soft noises as she moves. As she nods along with THE FINGERLESS

LADY's story, the exotic jewelry fills my head with sounds reminiscent of foreign bazaars.[1]

"One evening toward the end of our trip, as I lay in the dark of my tent listening to the Gray Jays singing a few late-night songs, I realized something as the majestic and varied images from the day's hike sifted beautifully through my mind." At this point THE FINGERLESS LADY leans forward, her eyes wide and encouraging. "God, it dawned on me, is like a mountain.

"God is like a mountain. And everyone has a different perspective of God. We all stand in different places, upon different ground. And every religion represents a different side of the mountain. Those people who are born on the south side of the mountain have one view of the mountain, and those born on the north may talk about God in completely different ways. And it wouldn't be unheard of—would it?—for the North People and the South People to point fingers at each other and argue about who was right about the mountain." CONFLICT IS ALWAYS HORRIBLE and PERSPECTIVE IS EVERYTHING exchange knowing looks and smile at THE FINGERLESS LADY, encouraging her.

"But when it comes right down to it, north or south, we're all just talking about the same mountain. It turns out we're all right. We're all right!"

At this point she puts both hands up—thumbs pointed up, scarred stubs sitting there, impotent.

A huge, encouraging smile is on her face.

"Buddhism sees one side of God. And Christianity sees another side of God. And Islam is a different perspective altogether.

"One person may see expansive white glaciers. Someone else may see sharp rocks and tall cliffs. Another may see only moss and ferns and feathery waterfalls.

"What's most important is that we recognize that we all have a different perspective. That we embrace the varied nature of our perspectives.

"We are *all* right! Every idea about God is a right idea about God!"

Here she is actually standing up, filled with excitement, flashing her stubby thumbs-up to every idea in the living room of my head. Her smile, her Barney-worthy smile, shines encouragement to all around her. Her story usually ends with this all-embracing gesture, this energy, this enthusiasm.

NO THROWING IDEAS

After telling her story, THE FINGERLESS LADY tends to get emotional and starts to walk around the living room of my head, hugging every idea she comes near, whispering what I presume to be encouraging words in their ears.

While she roams and hugs and nods and whispers, there's usually silence. Most of the ideas living up in my head aren't accustomed to being hugged. Many of them like it, though. They aren't used to being affirmed when they haven't even told their story. THE FINGERLESS LADY offers an odd, warm sort of acceptance that many of the ideas up in my head take to just fine.

Eventually a din of conversation starts to rise as the other ideas in my head respond to her story and ask questions about her "truth" about mountains and perspectives and all. CONFLICT IS ALWAYS HORRIBLE usually comes out from his corner to shout words of encouragement to her. He loves her story. And his vocal enthusiasm is notable because he usually stays hidden during meetings in the living room of my head. After all, the living room is a place designed for engagement among ideas, and to him and his allergy toward conflict, engagement is a scary prospect. But THE FINGERLESS LADY, with her hugs, brings him out of hiding and encourages him. *Maybe,* I see him thinking, *there won't be a need for any more conflict.*

"You see," he says with tears coming down his face, "there is a better way. A way to live without awkwardness and disagreements. A way to live without hurtful comments and awkward silences. A way to live in harmony. Harmony and respect and acceptance. Just look at this idea and the hugs she is giving out. Why aren't more ideas like this? Why aren't more ideas so accepting and welcoming and . . . And why can't we just all get along?" CONFLICT IS ALWAYS HORRIBLE catches himself and feels a bit awkward speaking with such volume around other ideas. His eyes drop and his face flushes. "I just like her," he says as he takes his seat again, a smile still on his face.

THE BEAUTY OF NATURE and THE INHERENT WISDOM OF THAT WHICH IS POETIC exchange knowing looks and smile, both of them enthralled with her story as well. THE BEAUTY OF NATURE is absolutely beaming. And THE INHERENT WISDOM

OF THAT WHICH IS POETIC throws his two cents into the ring.

"It just makes sense, doesn't it? It absolutely resonates with nature and life." THE INHERENT WISDOM OF THAT WHICH IS POETIC struggles for words. He always seems to have more energy and passion than words. He ends his short attempt at a speech and just closes his eyes and nods. He looks like he's meditating. And the rest of the ideas in my head aren't sure what they're supposed to say next.

While CONFLICT IS ALWAYS HORRIBLE and THE BEAUTY OF NATURE and others are perked up by THE FINGERLESS LADY's story, there are some other ideas that aren't so impressed with her story.

The loudest of them is usually EXISTENTIALISM. EXISTENTIALISM is a rough, dirty, emotional idea with a fancy name not befitting his grubby appearance. EXISTENTIALISM is given to impassioned speeches, and all of the ideas in my head take notice when he throws himself into a living room discussion.

EXISTENTIALISM brushes his messy hair out of his eyes and gazes from where he's sitting over to THE FINGERLESS LADY, who's now sitting in the middle of the living room. His voice is rough, like the voice of someone who's been sleeping outside for too many nights in a row. "But wait a second. Rocks are rocks, right?"

The rest of the ideas in my head quiet down, not

sure if they are supposed to answer this question or what the answer would be.

EXISTENTIALISM continues in his abrupt voice. "Rocks are rocks. There's no question about that. It doesn't matter what part of a mountain you are on—a rock is a rock. And on no part of the mountain would you . . . *eat* a rock, let's say. Would you?"

More silence. THE FINGERLESS LADY looks uncomfortable with EXISTENTIALISM's dirty face and harsh voice. He tends to spit a little as he talks, and she notices this.

EXISTENTIALISM—not one to waste time on a podium—finishes his point. "Rocks are rocks. And cliffs are cliffs. Bears are bears. Edible plants are edible plants. And the height of the mountain is the height of the mountain. Whether you can see the summit or not, whether there's a thick cloud cover or not, the mountain *is* a certain height at its summit. The summit *is* that height, no matter where you stand on the mountain. Don't you see? Mount Rainier exists. It exists. And that means something, lady."

EXISTENTIALISM is getting excited now, his wild hair flying as he gestures to the ideas sitting around him, his spit getting on a few of the ideas sitting closest to him in the living room up in my head. "This Mountain Analogy thrusts absolutes into our faces! This Mountain Analogy insists on nonnegotiable, hard realities. A mountain is not relative at all, and no one hiking around it—no matter what side of the mountain they are on—will think that jumping off a cliff is not inherently dangerous or that eating poisonous berries and rocks for dinner is a good idea!"

THE INHERENT WISDOM OF THAT WHICH IS POETIC starts nodding slowly at this point. Meanwhile, THE FINGERLESS LADY has an incredulous, offended look on her face, as if someone in the room had farted. You can tell she's not used to keeping such company.

EXISTENTIALISM is preaching now and ends with volume. "Face it, everyone. Any analogy you take from this earth, this dirt- and rock- and tree- and blood- and flesh-filled earth, will insist on reality. The cosmos is hard. It exists. It is not negotiable!"

The living room reverberates with his last words and he sits down, the adrenaline of debate coursing through his body. His face stares around at the ideas near him, his eyes full of energy. He wipes his mouth with the back of his sleeve.

At this point THE FINGERLESS LADY walks over to EXISTENTIALISM. When she speaks, her voice is still controlled and calm but has a subtle edge to it. She looks down at him where he sits and says, "But the spiritual realm is different. God is not like a rock. God is spirit. He is relationship. He is love. He is not like a mountain of *rocks*. He is like a mountain of . . . *God*."

EXISTENTIALISM smiles (and it is a genuine smile; he always seems to have a good time). "So God is negotiable? OK. But what makes you think that the metaphysical or spiritual realm would behave any differently than the physical realm? What would lead you to dismiss the basic structure and rhythm and DNA of what exists in the physical world when you begin speaking of that which is spiritual?"

THE FINGERLESS LADY continues to smile calmly down at him. "Because it is just that—*spiritual*. God *transcends* the physical. He goes above and beyond the laws of this world. That's why he is God."

She looks down at EXISTENTIALISM with a look that makes him think she's about to lean over and offer him a hug. He shrugs his shoulders. "But just because something exists in an invisible and nonphysical way, it doesn't necessarily follow that it operates by a completely different set of rules than does the rest of the cosmos. Nothing in creation is negotiable—things are what they are. Meaning derives from stuff. 'No ideas, but in things,' right?[1] So why necessarily assume that, when it comes to God, all of a sudden reality is negotiable? Makes no sense, lady. If God exists, then he exists. He is."

"But that is exactly my point: God *is* God." Her smile widens; her voice continues to flow calmly.

"It is we humans who have such a limited perspective on him. We can only see a little bit of this very real God. My limited perspective on God is not God. God is God."

THE FINGERLESS LADY looks over at her good friend PERSPECTIVE IS EVERYTHING and nods as she continues. "Which is why no humans should try to shove their limited view of God onto other people. There's no reason to be throwing our ideas at each other. Our posture should be one of *acceptance*. To recognize, in humility, that our perspective of the mountain is not the *only* perspective. And that someone seeing a different part of the mountain is being true to his or her perspective. We must not throw our ideas at others. That only creates division and arrogance." PERSPECTIVE IS EVERYTHING nods in agreement, the foreign sound of exotic jewelry wafting through my mind.

THE FINGERLESS LADY up in my head lifts her head proudly, building up a steam of words and passion. "Just look around this world, and wherever you find violence and war, you will see at the core of that mess one thing: *intolerance*." (She says this word hesitantly, as if it's a cuss word of the worst order.) "How does this aggressive, arrogant, religiously zealous posture help anything? It only causes disagreements and arguments and eventually war. Yes, war!"

Her eyes are now wide and obviously concerned as she continues. "The only real enemies these days are the zealots, those who arrogantly hold to a narrow-minded, myopic view of God and insist that their perspective is *the* perspective. They insensitively dismiss all other perspectives and blindly insist that their own view of the mountain is the first and last word on the subject. And as if this weren't bad enough, they take these beliefs and throw them at anyone who comes near them. Those who thoughtlessly throw their ideas at others are the cause of so much of the unnecessary strife and pain that exist on this world of ours.

"Their conversations are not civil; they are aggressive and rude and combative. They shove their ideas into the mouths of others with force. They use their own ideas as swords, as weapons to destroy the ideas of others."

THE FINGERLESS LADY looks down at EXISTENTIALISM with a hint of pity in her eyes. "We're not in the Dark Ages anymore, you know. Why can't we all just hold our own small perspectives dear to our hearts and allow other people to do the same? Maybe I learn about expansive white glaciers and you learn about calm little valleys, whereas someone else learns about sharp rocks on cliffs."

EXISTENTIALISM looks up at the lady with a confused look on his face. The lady returns his gaze and raises her voice slightly, as if chanting a motto that will ignite a crowd. "It's the composite picture that's most true!"

At this THE INHERENT TRUTH OF THAT WHICH FITS ON A BUMPER STICKER (a close relative of THE INHERENT TRUTH OF THAT WHICH IS POETIC) can't hold his place anymore. He is so excited about what he's hearing that he jumps up and starts spouting short phrases. He is like a machine gun of philosophy. "God is too big to fit in one religion! God doesn't discriminate, only religions do! If you believe you can tell me what to think, I believe I can tell you where to go!" He looks around with a huge smile on his face.

But in the living room in my head there is only a smattering of applause at this. A few ideas repeat some of his bumper sticker phrases, looking impressed and smiling. But mostly there are confused looks and a few ideas that raise their hands, looking like they have something to say.

EXISTENTIALISM is one of the ideas that looks like he has something to say, but another idea stands up first and addresses THE FINGERLESS LADY. This new idea, THE BRILLIANCE OF COLLABORATION, looks both excited and concerned. She motions to THE FINGERLESS LADY and says, "But it's only powerful, it's only *composite,* if we actually talk with each other. If we are willing to talk and debate and discuss and disagree and correct each other. That's what collaboration is all about. Isn't that right?"

"*Correct* each other?" THE FINGERLESS LADY

looks offended. "But that's exactly what we *shouldn't* be doing. How can we ever point our fingers at someone else?" She looks down at her hands, her right thumb rubbing the nubs on her left hand. She is lost in her thoughts for a moment and then looks up, seeming even more confident than before. "How can we ever say someone is *wrong*?" She flinches as she says this word. "We are each seeing the mountain from our own perspective, which is a *valid perspective*. Every view, every idea is valid."

THE BRILLIANCE OF COLLABORATION shakes her head thoughtfully. "Yes, but the whole point is coming together to share our ideas, so that we each get a better, more nuanced, more collaborative idea than we could ever come up with ourselves. Right? Only through talking and discussing and disagreeing and debating can we have any hope of really seeing the mountain clearly. Talking is beautiful. Sharing ideas is wonderful. But the point of conversation isn't just display. Sharing our ideas isn't like giving someone a hands-off tour of inert, fragile specimens in a museum. Our ideas aren't just for passive display. The point of conversation is to gain and learn and be corrected and . . . collaborate!"[2]

THE FINGERLESS LADY frowns, but THE BRILLIANCE OF COLLABORATION continues. "Just think about it. There could be someone who is caught in a fog on the mountain and can't see a thing. Or maybe someone is sitting in a valley, staring at a false summit, and assumes (as we all would) that it is the true summit of the mountain. Or what if someone wanders off and is looking at a totally different mountain—and is sending back data to the rest of us that doesn't mesh with what we've seen about the right mountain at all!"

"But we can't say that any one perspective of the mountain is better or worse—"

"Why not?" THE BRILLIANCE OF COLLABORATION interrupts THE FINGERLESS LADY. "If we really are talking with each other and gaining perspective on the mountain, when we try to put the pieces together, that will necessarily involve correcting some people. That's the power of a composite view. That's what taking each other seriously leads to.

"We collaborate about the mountain because some people might get caught in a cave and forget all about sunlight or trees or flowing water. If they become convinced that all the world is a cave, then we can talk with them and correct them. *Not* all the world is a cave."

THE FINGERLESS LADY looks back at THE BRILLIANCE OF COLLABORATION with a smirk on her face. "But you are just assuming the world is not a cave because you've never seen that perspective. It is the utmost arrogance to assume you can point to someone and outright dismiss what she sees as *invalid* and affirm what *you* see as perfectly clear!"

"And maybe, just maybe all the world *is* a cave. For them." This last contribution is uttered in a mysterious voice. A smooth, feminine voice full of intrigue and wisdom and seduction. It's a voice full of intellectual flirt, and it comes from ME AND MY REALITY. This idea often follows THE FINGERLESS LADY around. I see them together often, though ME AND MY REALITY isn't usually quite so bold up in my head as THE FINGERLESS LADY is.

Usually she just sits back and makes eyes with other ideas. I've seen her winking a time or two at THE INHERENT WISDOM OF THAT WHICH IS POETIC. She's definitely a Sexy Idea, and so when she does stand up and throw in with THE FINGERLESS LADY, it really turns up the heat in the living room up in my head.[3]

Chapter 4

POINTING IS RUDE

ME AND MY REALITY is wearing a little black dress and she slinks around my head with the ease that some women carry with them. Even though we're right in the middle of THE FINGERLESS LADY's story, ME AND MY REALITY commands the attention of other ideas up in my head, and THE FINGERLESS LADY doesn't mind at all if she steps in for a while.

"You seem to be pretty stuck on the idea that we need to come to some consensus view of this one mighty mountain." ME AND MY REALITY looks over at THE BRILLIANCE OF COLLABORATION with a twinkle in her eye. "But what if there isn't just one mountain? What if we are each seeing a different mountain?"

EXISTENTIALISM looks up sharply from where he's sitting with his messy hair and dirty hands, a confused look on his face. THE FINGERLESS LADY smiles as she looks around at the confused, almost spellbound ideas in the living room up in my head.

"Did you know," ME AND MY REALITY says, shooting a glance at THE BEAUTY OF NATURE, "that when two people are standing next to each other and looking at a rainbow, they are actually seeing two different rainbows?"

Gasps erupt from various ideas that are now leaning in, listening to ME AND MY REALITY's smooth voice. "What we call a 'rainbow' is actually the specific refraction of light off rain or mist that we see exactly where we are standing. Two feet over? It's a completely different thing you are looking at."

PERSPECTIVE IS EVERYTHING and THE FINGERLESS LADY exchange knowing looks, grins evident on their faces. ME AND MY REALITY continues, "The plain fact is that there is no singular, autonomous rainbow. We each *create* a rainbow based on where we are standing. Our perspective brings our own rainbow into existence by being there to receive those specific, unique beams of light coming at us."

At this point PERSPECTIVE IS EVERYTHING is nearly floating, an engaged, puppylike look on her big eyes as she stares over at this new, sexy idea. THE INHERENT WISDOM OF THAT WHICH IS POETIC is likewise entranced.

ME AND MY REALITY smiles attractively, motioning with her elegant arms. "And doesn't it make sense that this is how it works with 'God' or 'truth' or 'the mountain'? Perhaps the reason people see things differently is that they are actually seeing different things."

There is a pregnant pause in my mind at this point. Many of the other ideas stare, entranced. But EXISTENTIALISM is still scratching his head, his face scrunched up like he's smelled something bad and is trying to figure out what it is. And one old idea, a frail idea that looks like he might fall over, stands up slowly and makes his painful way over to a stool near where ME AND MY REALITY is standing.

The official name of this old idea is THE AU-THORITY OF SCRIPTURE, but up in my head he goes by the name THE OLD MAN CLUTCHING THE BIG BLACK BIBLE. Or just THE OLD MAN. This old-fashioned idea carries around a huge black book in his frail arms and rarely says much of anything without reading from that book of his.[1]

The ideas in my head wait patiently for THE OLD MAN to get settled. He's a Permanent Resident, af-ter all, and ME AND MY REALITY, though she's not used to being around such an old, weak-looking idea, can tell that he has seniority up in my head. She waits patiently.

"Young lady," THE OLD MAN starts speaking, having to clear his throat a time or two as he goes along, like knocking rust from an old piece of metal, "I beg to differ. It is not like that with God or Truth or most things in reality. They are there. God is there. Truth exists outside of us. Singular and approachable. And knowable."

ME AND MY REALITY opens her mouth to respond but sees the other ideas staying silent. She wonders why such an idea would be given such prominence in my head, but she holds her tongue out of respect.

THE OLD MAN continues, tapping the cover of the book with his old, vein-covered hand, "The Truth is. It exists. And in these pages you can read about the Truth being received, being rejected, twisted, spurned, handled, wandered away from, repeated, embraced, heralded and so on. But it is a thing. Something real outside of us. Reality is. And we interact with it."

"I'm sorry, but . . ." ME AND MY REALITY has held her tongue long enough and is ready to hear a smooth, attractive voice fill the living room in my head again. "But how can any one person claim to know the truth? It's like a rainbow. We all stand—"

"Young lady, there is such a man."

As THE OLD MAN catches his breath, YOUTH-FUL CYNICISM, his straight, dark bangs covering his bored eyes, shakes his head. "Oh no, here he goes."

THE OLD MAN glances at YOUTHFUL CYNICISM with what appears to be a slight smile and looks back at ME AND MY REALITY, standing with her well-manicured hands defiantly placed on her hips. You can tell she's not used to being interrupted.

"There is indeed such a man. Jesus himself, right here in just this one Gospel, said 'I tell you the truth' thirty times.[2] It's like he couldn't open his mouth without announcing what was about to happen as he spoke: he was going to speak Truth. With a capital T."

YOUTHFUL CYNICISM rolls his eyes, but THE OLD MAN continues. "It was said of Jesus that he came full of grace and Truth.[3] Overflowing with Truth, he was. Because he had come from God. He had received truth from God and was—"

"Listen, old-timer. I get your point." ME AND MY REALITY's hands are off her hips and moving passionately again. "But old myths and chants about truth from ancient times are irrelevant. Did you know, for example, that if you consider the findings of quantum physics carefully, you will find that different people are actually experiencing different realities?"

She looks down at THE OLD MAN sitting on his stool and feels a little pity for using such advanced words around him. "There's not one large, independent mountain out there to be looked at. We each create our own little mountain. And so how foolish, how naive to glance over at others living genuinely and peacefully on their own mountain of reality and point at them and declare, from your perspective, that they are 'lost' or 'wrong' or 'misguided.' They are just on a different mountain."

THE OLD MAN furrows his brow, his hands tenderly holding the large Bible in his lap. EXISTENTIALISM is scratching his messy hair, and his eyebrows have the look of someone who's trying to follow a foreign language he doesn't know very well. THE BRILLIANCE OF COLLABORATION stands still, not seeming to know what to say either.

ME AND MY REALITY continues, her voice growing softer, as if she is whispering into someone's ear. Someone who likes the whispering as much for the feel of breath on the ear as for the content of the whisper. "Enlightened and peaceful living means being at peace within your own reality and coexisting in peace with others who are on their own little mountains. We need not bother ourselves with pointing and archaic labels such as 'lost.' We are all living genuinely in our own, self-constructed realities."

ME AND MY REALITY looks pleased with herself, but jumps in shock when a nearly indescribably dirty and *frightening* idea stands up abruptly right next to her!

This idea is all dirt and grime, and there even seems to be some dried blood on his face. All of the ideas in my head fall silent before this idea. His name is TRAGEDY.

TRAGEDY speaks into the living room in my head with a piercing, tired voice. "Listen, lady. People get lost on mountains all the time. There is nothing arrogant about recognizing that."

ME AND MY REALITY tries smiling, but her eyes look terrified of this dangerous-looking idea. "But how can you use the word 'lost'? What if—"

"When I say lost, I mean lost. Have you ever met a pedophile?" TRAGEDY stares at ME AND MY REALITY.

"Excuse me?!" ME AND MY REALITY obviously doesn't like being interrupted and talked to in this manner. She also looks confused by TRAGEDY's question.

TRAGEDY looks her in the eyes, no expression on his face. "Have you ever met a pedophile? I have. And pedophiles are absolutely convinced that having sex with small kids is perfectly fine. Some of them really believe that."

There is silence in my head at this point. A meaningful silence. TRAGEDY looks over at ME AND MY REALITY and fills the silence. "Unless you are ready to hug everyone and give everyone a stamp of approval—and I mean *everyone*—then you have to admit that some people are wrong. Just wrong. They've gotten lost. There's something in their precious perspective that's twisted.

"People get lost on mountains all the time. And end up with the strangest conclusions. Pointing fingers isn't arrogant. It's realistic."

ME AND MY REALITY looks offended, indignant.

She stares, blinking, around the living room of ideas in my head like an elegant princess who has somehow accidentally ended up in a bowling alley. She stares at TRAGEDY as if faced with a monster and then looks around as if expecting either the other ideas to contradict him or me to kick him out of my head.

But I don't kick him out. And BLESSED POVERTY O' SPIRIT sighs and nods, calling out from her corner of the room, "We all deserve to have some fingers pointed at us." And I can see that THE DIRTY BEGGAR living in my head, who is hiding in a far corner of the living room, starts to nod his bowed head.[4]

And so usually she walks right on out of my head. ME AND MY REALITY, that is.

You can tell she just can't stand to be under the same roof with some of these ideas, especially that TRAGEDY guy. So she just leaves. Ideas do that sometimes. My head is like a house, after all. And some folks just can't get along and live together. ME AND MY REALITY and TRAGEDY are two such ideas.

But THE FINGERLESS LADY isn't through yet. You can see determination in her face. And you can see how some of the other ideas up in my head like her. She stands for love, after all. And TRAGEDY is so harsh, and this pointing of fingers that he advocates is so violent and hurtful. THE FINGERLESS LADY is on a mission and believes in her story.

She won't look TRAGEDY in the eye but speaks to the other ideas around her. "But what he is advocating is inherently harmful!" THE FINGERLESS LADY has grown more passionate than before. Her voice is still mostly in control, but she is starting to motion strongly with her arms. She even begins to point at TRAGEDY with her left thumb from time to time to emphasize certain words. "Ideas aren't weapons! We can't just shove our ideas at others and dismiss their ideas as nonsense. Pointing fingers are the ugliest things possible on this earth of ours. They should be cut off—they should! Getting rid of these ugly, malicious pointing fingers is well worth the pain it causes to chop them off. To say that humans should go around picking out people and pointing at them is to advocate hate speech and arrogance and religious wars and—"

THE BRILLIANCE OF COLLABORATION is smiling now, looking interested in what THE FINGERLESS LADY is saying. "So you think he's wrong, do you? You don't like the story he's telling?"

"His arrogance is hate-filled and old-fashioned and medieval and—"

"And . . . *not right*?" THE BRILLIANCE OF COLLABORATION looks THE FINGERLESS LADY in the eye.

"It's *absolutely* not right."

THE BRILLIANCE OF COLLABORATION nods at

the woman and then motions to the ideas surrounding them. "Which is why we come here to the living room to interact as ideas, right? To tell our stories, to discuss, to disagree. That's what thinking is: us working it all out in the living room. It's TRAGEDY telling you he thinks your story is flawed. And it's you telling him you think his story is flawed. That's how thinking happens. And that's why we talk with others about our ideas. Sure, ideas aren't weapons to use aggressively in debate. But they're also not specimens to be displayed like an off-limits relic behind a velvet rope barrier at a museum. Ideas are meant to interact. That's the whole point."

EXISTENTIALISM rises up again, his eyes aflame. He points over at TRAGEDY and says, "Pedophiles exist, right? They actually exist. And he thinks that pedophiles believe terrible stories. That they are just flat-out wrong. But that's because there's an experience he's drawing from—real, rock-hard stories and experiences. That's where ideas come from, from real stuff. Now, I'm not sure what I believe about God, but I sure can tell you that *if* he is, then he is what he is. He exists. And that's something we can talk about and discuss and disagree about and—"

At that point THE FINGERLESS LADY will often leave.

She will walk right out of my head and join ME

AND MY REALITY on a sidewalk somewhere. There they can lick their wounds and together ridicule this head of mine and the odd ideas I allow to stay up there.

THE FINGERLESS LADY, after all, is mostly used to visiting heads where she gets smiles and nods and is invited to stay—often as a Permanent Resident.[5] But in my head she gets a mixed reaction. She feels ganged up on. Which often makes her walk right on out.

But sometimes she does stay up in my head a bit longer. Her story is just poetic enough to please some of the ideas living in my head, and on some days she takes encouragement from THE INHERENT WISDOM OF THAT WHICH IS POETIC, THE INHERENT WISDOM OF THAT WHICH FITS ON A BUMPER STICKER, CONFLICT IS ALWAYS HORRIBLE, PERSPECTIVE IS EVERYTHING and others . . . and tries to stick it out.

She ultimately has a story of love and acceptance. And she knows that this is a story worth fighting for.

But the longer she stays up in my head, the more likely it becomes that THE OLD MAN living up there (that is, THE OLD MAN CLUTCHING THE BIG BLACK BIBLE) will want to ask her some questions. And that's always an interesting exchange to watch.

THE OLD MAN coughs a few times, then speaks, "Well, we're talking about God being a mountain and about humans having such limited perspectives on the mountain and about their need to talk with each other about the mountain—or *not* talk with each other, depending on your take on that."

THE FINGERLESS LADY jumps in. "Right. We all just have one perspective. We're limited by our time and place and where we're born and—"

"But what if there were someone who wasn't limited like that?" THE OLD MAN looks straight at THE FINGERLESS LADY. "What if there were someone who could fly! Who could range all over the mountain, see all sides of it, fly over the most dangerous parts, fly into the most tender valleys, examine the harsh peaks on the Tatoosh Range and sit atop the summit? What then?"

YOUTHFUL CYNICISM, lounging in a nearby couch, pipes up, "Let me guess, old-timer. You don't happen to be talking about *Jesus*, do you?" The ideas living in my head are used to YOUTHFUL CYNICISM's sarcastic jabs, especially at THE OLD MAN.

THE OLD MAN looks over at YOUTHFUL CYNICISM and seems pleased (the sarcasm lost on his old ears). "Why, yes, I am!"

YOUTHFUL CYNICISM sighs audibly. "Thrilling."

"What are you guys talking about?" THE FIN-

LISTENING TO
THE MOUNTAIN

THE OLD MAN CLUTCHING THE BIG BLACK BIBLE
stands up and walks between EXISTENTIALISM and
THE FINGERLESS LADY. He looks faint, as if he had
exerted himself too much. Once there's quiet between the two, THE OLD MAN sits down on his
stool again, breathing hard.

The other ideas wait for him to catch his
breath—he is a Permanent Resident in my head and
therefore gets more respect than the average idea
up there. After sitting for a moment to catch his
breath, he looks up at the fingerless woman and
EXISTENTIALISM and speaks in his ancient, feeble
voice. There's a polite smile on his face. "So, Miss,
I have a simple question: What if there were someone who could fly over the mountain?"

EXISTENTIALISM looks at THE OLD MAN with in-
terest in his eyes. "What do you mean, *fly* over the
mountain?"

GERLESS LADY looks genuinely lost.

YOUTHFUL CYNICISM pipes up again from his couch. "THE OLD MAN here thinks that Jesus was Superman and knew all sorts of things about the God Mountain that 'mere' humans can't know. Isn't that right?"

THE OLD MAN nods and starts flipping through the thin, faded pages of the large book on his lap. Stopping at a certain page, he begins reading slowly in his ancient, feeble voice, "No one has ever seen God, but the one and only, who is himself God and is in closest relationship with the Father, has made him known."[1]

YOUTHFUL CYNICISM brushes his bangs away from his eyes for a moment. "Listen, old-timer. We know about the myths people made up about Jesus. And we know that Jesus didn't hold the same views of himself that they did. He never flew anywhere. He just wanted to teach about love or something. It's folks later on who came up with the Superman myths about him."

THE OLD MAN looks at YOUTHFUL CYNICISM confused. "Oh, but Jesus claimed to be able to fly. One time he said, 'Very truly I tell you, we speak of what we know, and we testify to what we have seen, but still you people do not accept our testimony. I have spoken to you of earthly things and you do not believe; how then will you believe if I speak of heavenly things? No one has ever gone into heaven except the one who came from heaven—the Son of Man.' "[2]

"I'm confused," says THE FINGERLESS LADY. "Who's the 'Son of Man'?"

YOUTHFUL CYNICISM slouches down even further into his couch. "That's how Jesus referred to himself, apparently. I've heard this old man going off about Jesus so much. The old guy actually believes that Jesus was sent to earth by God."

THE OLD MAN looks over at YOUTHFUL CYNICISM. "If God is a mountain, as this lady suggests, then we're not limited to our little human perspectives. Jesus could fly all over the mountain. He was the Son of the Mountain. And mostly what he taught about *was* the mountain."

THE OLD MAN gazes down at the large book on his lap. "He said he came to tell people the truth about the mountain. To free them from their limited perspectives. In fact, he claimed that he talked to the mountain! One time he said, 'My teaching is not my own. It comes from the one who sent me.'[3] He claimed he was just passing on what the mountain said about itself."

"Well, I know that Jesus was a good teacher." THE FINGERLESS LADY smiles politely at THE OLD MAN, trying to sound encouraging. "He taught much about God and love. He is one of our greatest teachers. And I applaud you for embracing his teachings about the mountain, just as all religious people do all over the world with their great teachers. We must embrace all of these well-meaning, enlightened teachers who have greater perspective on the mountain."

"What are you talking about, young lady?" THE OLD MAN's voice sounds strained. "Jesus didn't just claim to have a nice view of the mountain; he claimed that he *was* the mountain!"

Here THE OLD MAN starts flipping through the ancient, thin, faded pages until he finds the one he is looking for. "In the beginning was the Word, and the Word was with God, and the Word was God. He was with God in the beginning."[4]

THE OLD MAN looks back up at THE FINGERLESS LADY. "In other words, in the beginning was Jesus and Jesus was with the mountain and Jesus *was* the mountain. Jesus never claimed to have a worthwhile perspective on God. He said things like 'I am the way and the truth and the life. No one comes to the Father except through me. If you really know me, you will know my Father as well. From now on, you do know him and have seen him.'"[5]

YOUTHFUL CYNICISM chuckles sarcastically. "Unbelievable. Every time you read that, I can't fathom how anyone would believe such an arrogant, misguided statement."

"By the way, young man, have I ever told you how some folks responded to Jesus right when he said that?"

"Ooh. Let me guess. Are you going to read from your precious book again?"

THE OLD MAN, smiling, looks down at the huge, old book on his lap and reads, "Philip said, 'Lord, show us the Father and that will be enough for us.' Jesus answered: 'Don't you know me, Philip, even after I have been among you such a long time? Anyone who has seen me has seen the Father. How can you say, 'Show us the Father'? Don't you believe that I am in the Father, and that the Father is in me? The words I say to you I do not speak on my own authority. Rather, it is the Father, living in me, who is doing his work."[6]

YOUTHFUL CYNICISM smiles back at THE OLD MAN. "I think I kind of like this Philip guy."

"Ah, Philip. He ended up a great man of faith. His story is told here—"

YOUTHFUL CYNICISM shakes his head. "Are we almost done here? I think THE OLD MAN is overdue for his nap."

THE OLD MAN looks back over to THE FINGER-LESS LADY. "So, what do you say? What if there were someone who could fly all over the mountain? Who was from the mountain? Who, in some mysterious way, *was* the mountain itself?"

THE FINGERLESS LADY shrugs. "And what about this hypothetical situation?"

"Well, if that fellow talked about the mountain a lot, and if he said things about the mountain that contradicted what a lot of other people were saying about the mountain, then wouldn't that free us from this free-market, thumbs-up approach to everything that is said about the mountain?" THE OLD MAN stares at THE FINGERLESS LADY.

Her smile is gone as she stares back. She doesn't look good without the smile. It makes her kindergarten-teacher dress look oddly out of place. "I'm not sure, sir, what to say. This is a pretty far-fetched hypothetical situation you are painting."

YOUTHFUL CYNICISM pipes up. "Far-fetched?! You're being generous, lady."

THE OLD MAN looks into THE FINGERLESS LADY's eyes. "But if it were true—if such a man did exist and his perspective on the mountain were different from most people's—you would have to point a finger somewhere, right? Either at him for being"—here THE OLD MAN swallows before proceeding—"a liar, an arrogant, misguided person. Or you'd have to point some fingers at other people, dismissing the parts of their perspective on the mountain that contradict what the Son of the Mountain said about the mountain."

THE OLD MAN pauses, looking at the woman across from him. "Pointing fingers is called for either way, wouldn't you think?"

THE FINGERLESS LADY just stares at THE OLD MAN. She's not used to being in a head with this ancient relic of an idea, especially in a head where he gets respect and actually gets to finish his sentences and read from that dusty old book of his.

She stares over at him and doesn't like him. Him or that odd, musty, old-man smell of his.

Chapter 6

THE POINTING THUMB

All of the ideas living in my head are into stories. They each have their own story to tell. And they each love to hear other stories—and respond. That's what ideas do. That's their nature. That's what thinking is all about, after all.

And so most ideas in my head will listen to everything that goes on in the living room. They listen to THE FINGERLESS LADY telling her story. They listen to EXISTENTIALISM's critique of her. They listen to her answers. And they even listen to THE OLD MAN CLUTCHING THE BIG BLACK BIBLE.

And they want to see how THE FINGERLESS LADY responds to this old man. Usually she just grows quiet though. She frowns at THE OLD MAN. And with a strain in her voice says something along these lines . . .

"The hypothetical situation you are describing is ridiculous. Just ridiculous. The truth is, people are humans—just humans—trying to see the mountain. And humans all have limited perspectives.

The idea that there'd be a Son of the Mountain who had special insight on the mountain is ridiculous. And it's that kind of arrogant, myopic, zealous belief that leads people to do the most hateful things."

THE BRILLIANCE OF COLLABORATION leans forward. "So you think THE OLD MAN's wrong, do you?"

"I think his strange beliefs don't fit into reality. And therefore there is no real answer. Of course, if there *were* a special God-man who had special insight, and if he *did* say things that happened to contradict what others were saying, then he would be right and they would be wrong. Of course. But that's not reality."

THE BRILLIANCE OF COLLABORATION eyes her as if waiting for her to say something else. When she doesn't, THE BRILLIANCE OF COLLABORATION says, "According to your perspective, right?"

THE FINGERLESS LADY looks around at the ideas in my head, a pleading look in her eyes. "Listen, THE OLD MAN spreads hatred. He encourages pointing fingers and the throwing of ideas at each other, which just leads to division and anger!"

She catches herself, takes a few deep breaths and continues more calmly. "But we must all, in humility, embrace the perspectives we each have. We must. We are all right in our own ways. And if we embrace each other, we will be unified in love as we encircle this great mountain of God."

Sometimes the conversation in the living room up in my head goes on even further. But sometimes it just ends here.

There's something poetic and open and humble about THE FINGERLESS LADY's story. And as I travel around this great big world of ours, and look into different people's eyes, I like her story. I like what she says about understanding and not pointing and, especially, avoiding conflict with others. There is something beautifully hospitable about her, even though her voice is a little too sugary for my tastes.

But when I talk with the pedophile I know or watch the latest tragedy on the news, her story deflates terribly. It doesn't sound quite right anymore. And the look on her face when she's responding to EXISTENTIALISM doesn't sit well with me either. I like EXISTENTIALISM and how he asks rooted, earth-based questions. And her inability to engage with him sits awkwardly with me.

And, in the end, her inability to engage with THE OLD MAN and his big black Bible is most disconcerting. He is a Permanent Resident in my head— for reasons I've outlined in another tour of my head. And so her inability to engage with him for long leaves me feeling painfully uncomfortable with her and her story. Especially when she starts pointing at him with those two thumbs of hers, trying to get across the point that pointing fingers at others is not the thing to do.

Too much irony for me to handle usually. And too much tension for her under the same roof with all those other ideas.

Which means THE FINGERLESS LADY usually ends up leaving my head. Or getting kicked out by some other ideas. Or by me. Her story is just too thin and unsatisfying to me in the end. And there are other stories that make more sense to me. I don't feel right simply displaying my ideas like an intellectual flasher or staring at others' ideas like some voyeur. I think ideas are meant to interact.

I am a huge fan of ideas engaging each other, and her story doesn't allow space for that. Not for thoughtful engagement. And that leaves her story seeming unattractive. Makes me think her story doesn't have much truth to it. Yeah, truth.

I suppose this is what it means for me to believe in "truth." I know that some ideas just can't get along. And I don't mind being honest about that. I want to talk about these tensions among ideas. I want to be honest about these tensions, not ignore them like a dysfunctional family might ignore the alcoholic in the room.

It's this kind of honest dialogue, this pursuit of having a mind full of the best ideas out there, that is deep within me. I have a hunger for good stories. For real and honest and comprehensive stories. My upstairs aches for good stories. It aches for truth.

And so, if believing in truth and being hungry for thoughtfully engaging ideas means kicking this lady and her gospel of tolerance out of my head, then that's just fine.

Regardless of what I feel about her, or how uncomfortable she is up in my head with all those ideas I like up there, she'll come back. I know she will. Even if it's just to visit my head. You see, she's a popular lady these days—she and her fingerless thumbs-up gestures.

Almost everywhere I turn, whether reading a book or listening to the radio or just talking with my neighbors, she's right there telling her story and climbing back into my head.

....

CONCLUSION:
YOUR HEAD

....

If your head works anything like mine, then by your reading this book, THE FINGERLESS LADY has walked right into your head as well. Ideas are like that: like people who come into your head and interact with all the other ideas living there. So, um . . . THE FINGERLESS LADY's living in your head now too. Or at least visiting.

Maybe you're ready to kick her out right now. Maybe you hear the whistles and barked comments from some of the other ideas in your mind already. Maybe you really like her story. Maybe you gave her Permanent Resident status in your head long ago. Whatever the case, my advice is this: let the ideas in your head work it out.

Let them tell each other their stories. Pepper *them all* with questions. And see how things shake out.

That's what we've been given brains for, after

all. To think. To let the ideas work it out as we bring them all into the living room of our minds and ask them to interact with each other.

But remember, it's your head. It's your house of living ideas. No one in there gets to boss other ideas around—without your permission. No one gets to stay, no one has to leave, without your say-so.

So work it out. This is the job of humans—to philosophize, to think, to be in charge of our heads. THE FINGERLESS LADY has gone and walked right into the house of your head. She's in there now. It's up to you to figure out what to do with her.

It's your head, after all.

NOTES

introduction: my head

[1]To get a more comprehensive view of how things work up in my head, you'd have to read *All the Ideas Living in My Head: One Guy's Musings About Truth,* where I give a full tour of my upstairs and how thinking tends to go on up there. It's a tell-all about how ideas behave in my head, the different types of ideas there are, why certain ideas get special privileges, how my mind interacts with my heart and soul, how I talk with others about their ideas and what, exactly, I think about McDonald's French fries. Among other things.

chapter 2: the fingerless lady's story

[1]PERSPECTIVE IS EVERYTHING is a fascinating idea to spend time with in this globally minded world we live in. She often speaks up in my head these days, as you can see in chapter five of *The Old Man Living in My Head: One Guy's Musings About the Bible.*

chapter 3: no throwing ideas

[1]EXISTENTIALISM loves the poetry of William Carlos Williams and quotes him often. Other ideas think that such basic, ordinary, stuff-of-life images are absent of deep meaning. But EXISTENTIALISM can't get enough of the stuff.

²In my head there are three distinct ways of talking with others about our ideas: Waging Gang War, Visiting a Museum and Introducing Our Families. To Wage Gang War, we load up our ideas and shoot them at each other (violent but exciting). In Visiting a Museum we display our ideas (a sort of intellectual flashing) but don't allow touching. The best way, though, is letting our ideas interact with each other. I call this Introducing Our Families and talk more about it in chapter six of *All the Ideas Living in My Head: One Guy's Musings About Truth*.

³Ah, Sexy Ideas. These are a certain class of ideas that tend to affect me in a certain way. Namely, they come from the newest book or newest thinker of the day and have a sort of swagger and new-car smell that makes them quite convincing—even before I hear their story. See chapter four of *All the Ideas Living in My Head*.

chapter 4: pointing is rude

¹THE OLD MAN is strange enough, and has been a Permanent Resident of my head long enough, to warrant a closer look. I provide such a look in *The Old Man Living in My Head: One Guy's Musings About the Bible*.

²There are four Gospels in the Bible. Each of them tells the story of Jesus. In Matthew alone we see Jesus preface his comments thirty separate times by saying, "I tell you the truth . . ." and then telling what he wanted to tell.

³For example, this is said in John 1:14, 17.

⁴THE DIRTY BEGGAR is a fascinating, dark idea. I've given him a whole book to tell his story and explain why he is always so bent over and dirty: *The Dirty Beggar Living in My Head: One Guy's Musings About Evil and Hell*.

⁵Some ideas are so strong, and I like them so much, that

I give them special status as Permanent Residents. This doesn't mean they can never be kicked out of my head or at least be disagreed with, but it does mean they hold more sway up there in my head. For more on this, see chapters four through six of *All the Ideas Living in My Head: One Guy's Musings About Truth*.

chapter 5: listening to the mountain
[1]John 1:18
[2]John 3:11-13
[3]John 7:16
[4]John 1:1-2
[5]John 14:6-7
[6]John 14:8-10

ONE GUY'S HEAD SERIES

A bunch of ideas are running around in Don Everts's head. Some are permanent residents. Others are visitors, just passing through. When they all get together, some odd things start happening.

LIKEWISE. *Go and do.*

....

A man comes across an ancient enemy, beaten and left for dead. He lifts the wounded man onto the back of a donkey and takes him to an inn to tend to the man's recovery. Jesus tells this story and instructs those who are listening to "go and do likewise."

Likewise books explore a compassionate, active faith lived out in real time. When we're skeptical about the status quo, Likewise books challenge us to create culture responsibly. When we're confused about who we are and what we're supposed to be doing, Likewise books help us listen for God's voice. When we're discouraged by the troubled world we've inherited, Likewise books encourage us to hold onto hope.

In this life we will face challenges that demand our response. Likewise books face those challenges with us so we can act on faith.

....

likewisebooks.com

....